W [illegible] way

Kathy Lee and Roma Bishop

Little EAGLE

One night long ago,
some wise men in a far-off land
saw a bright new star in the sky.

'This star means that somewhere on earth
a baby king has been born,
a very special baby,' they said to each other.
'We must visit him.'

So each of them chose a present for the baby.
Then they set out, following the star.
Night after night they travelled onwards.
At last they came to Jerusalem,
where King Herod lived.

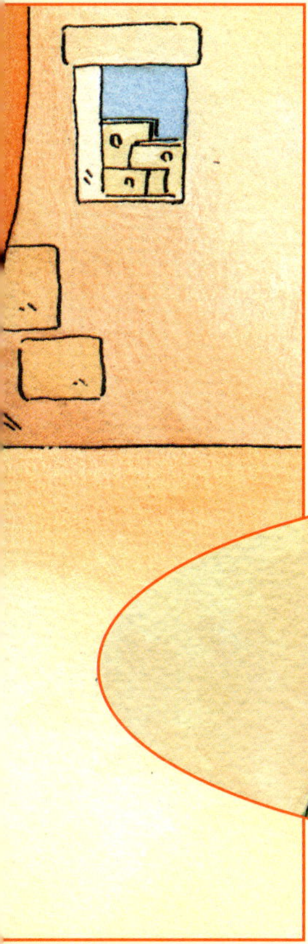

'Where is the baby king?' they asked.
'We saw his star in the sky.'
King Herod tried to look pleased,
but he was angry.
People might think that this new baby
should be the king of Jerusalem instead of him.

King Herod called together his own wise men.
'What do you know about a baby king?'
he asked.

‘Years ago, God promised that a special child
who will become a great leader
would be born in Bethlehem,’ they replied.

King Herod asked to see the visitors again.
'Go to Bethlehem,' he said.
'If you find the child, come back and tell me.'
He was secretly thinking of a plan
to get rid of this new king.

The wise men set out again
on their weary camels.
In the town of Bethlehem,
right above a house,
the star stood still in the sky.
They had come to the end of their journey.

The wise men went into the house.
They found the baby with Mary, his mother.
His name was Jesus.

Jesus had been born in a stable, not a palace.
But the wise men knew that he was someone special.
They knelt down to worship Jesus.

At last they had found the baby king.
The wise men were so happy!

They gave him their presents –
shining gold,
sweet frankincense
and costly myrrh.

In a dream that night,
God told the wise men not to go back
to King Herod, so they went home a different way.

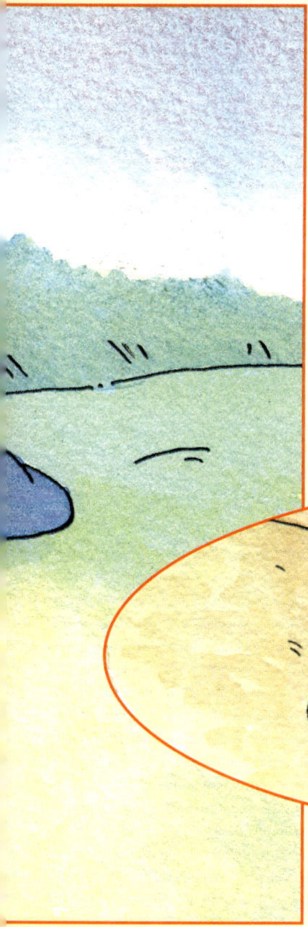

They set off for home joyfully,
glad they had made the long journey,
because they had seen Jesus, the baby king.

This story can be found
in the Bible in Matthew 2:1-12

Published in the UK by Eagle Publishing
PO Box 530, Guildford, Surrey GU2 4FH
ISBN 0 86347 435 7

First edition 2001

Printed and bound in Malta